THE HUNTING-HORN

BY

L. C. R. CAMERON

British Library Cataloguing-in-Publication Data
A catalogue record for this book is available from the
British Library

CONTENTS

Julia Margaret Cameron

Julia Margaret Cameron was born in Calcutta, India in 1815. Her father was a British official of the East India Company and her mother the daughter of French aristocrats. Cameron was educated in France, but returned to India, before moving to London, England with her husband in 1848.

In 1863, when Cameron was 48 years old, her daughter gave her a camera as a present. Within a year, Cameron became a member of the Photographic Societies of London and Scotland, and soon afterwards her fame began to spread. Alfred Lord Tennyson, her neighbour on the Isle of Wight, often brought friends to see her work and pose for pictures. Cameron's photography was marked by a laborious and careful process most unusual for her era.

The bulk of Cameron's photographs fall into two categories – closely framed portraits, and illustrative allegories based on famous religious and literary works. Amongst her portrait subjects were Charles Darwin, Alfred Lord Tennyson and Robert Browning. Her posed photographic illustrations, usually based on historical scenes or literary works, often took on the careful and rich quality of oil paintings.

Cameron's photographic career was short, spanning just eleven years, and while her work has had an impact on latter-day photographers, she was not widely appreciated in her day – as her great-niece, Virginia Woolf, would later lament. In 1875, Cameron to Ceylon (now Sri Lanka), where she continued her photography, but struggled to find the requisite chemicals. She died Kalutara, Ceylon in 1879, aged 64.

THE HUNTING-HORN:

WHAT TO BLOW

AND

HOW TO BLOW IT

I

THERE can be little doubt that one of the chief charms of the hunting-field, next after the actual cry of hounds, and possibly of the bright effect lent to the landscape by "pink" coats in winter, or by the blue and scarlet uniforms of the otter-hunter during the summer months, has ever been the inspiriting sound of the Horn, as its notes are borne on the breeze from the depths of some covert, echoed over the uplands as the chase goes gallantly forward, or come floating across the water of river or of lake.

And yet how few among modern Masters and huntsmen of hounds do anything save, as Colonel Anstruther-Thomson complained, "blow the same monotonous note on the Horn all day long without variation or meaning." Many men who can blow a Horn well enough, so far as getting a clear and sustained note from the tube at the proper moment without difficulty is concerned, have never learned so to vary the notes they employ as to convey a separate meaning by each of their calls, that shall be distinguishable to the ears of hounds and members of the field alike.

The reason for this deplorable state of things lies chiefly in the fact that no modern work on hunting deigns to give instruction in the notation of calls on the Hunting-horn, if we except the few and simple lessons contained in *Hints to Huntsmen* and *Otters and Otter-Hunting*. Even these books are of very little use to those, who, like the Master of one of the most famous of English packs, with whom I was recently in correspondence, are "quite ignorant of music in any shape or form."

It is, therefore, in order to remove this reproach from modern hunting literature, as well as to provide the proper notation of those "measures of blowing," as they were formerly called, which remain of practical utility in the hunting-field of to-day, together with the necessary simple instructions in the art of reading off the "music" of these measures, that I have conceived this little book.

It must not be forgotten that the original object of blowing the Horn was to enlighten the company as to the progress of the sport, not to direct the hounds. Indeed, in the collection of twenty-five "lessons" here presented, but three are intended for hounds, and of these two are of quite modern invention. The only ancient call used for this purpose was the Recheat in the simplest of its several forms; employed to recall hounds running a counter-scent, or to bring on tail hounds once the main body had got away with their quarry. To this day the information of the field is the principal object of Horn music with the three or four hundred packs that hunt in France and Belgium, where it is possible in the vast forests of those countries to keep in touch with hounds all day without seeing them, to recognise every point of venery, and to so regulate one's movements by the "lessons" blown as to miss none of the sport, and finally to be in at the death. In England, on the contrary, in a woodland country, the finest horseman and the keenest sportsman—one with an accurate knowledge of the country will often be thrown out at the beginning of the day and lose every chance of participation in the sport, because the Master or his huntsman are ignorant of any method of advising their followers as to what hounds are doing or are about to do.

II

The original Hunting-horn was of a curved pattern—being the actual horn of some beast, more or less ornamented with metal—sounding a single note. The Compassed Horn was introduced from France, where it still remains in use, and was so-called because it possessed a compass of twelve notes, from C below the line in the treble clef to G above the line. On this, elaborate "tunes" could, of course, be blown, and much of the modern French Horn-music is of quite an important character. This Horn, familiar to us in old pictures of the chase and in the modern orchestra, was so bent as to encircle the body of the wearer. It is never likely to come into fashion again in this country, so may be dismissed without further comment: though I append the fanfare of the present Duc de Chartres' hunt at Chantilly called *La D'Orleans: Fanfare de l'équipage*, as an interesting example of what can be done on the Compassed Horn. It will be noticed that it is arranged to be blown by two or four musicians in concert: a custom once prevalent in England, where at the death of certain quarry, after the "mort" or "pryse" had been duly sounded, such of the field as carried horns blew the appropriate Recheat in unison and immediately gave a general "Whoo-whoop."

The straight Horn came into vogue about the end of the seventeenth century; shortly after which the elevation of the fox to the front rank among beasts of chase brought about those changes in the sport of hunting which resulted in the gradual neglect of all points of venery, and finally in the decline of Horn-music almost to the vanishing point.

I have seen straight Horns made of boxwood and other substances; but, of course, those of metal are the only ones for practical purposes. They may be of copper with German silver mouthpieces and ferrules or bands; or of German silver throughout; or of copper, with mouthpiece and ferrule of sterling silver; and, of course, of sterling silver throughout. The orthodox length of the straight metal Horn at its first introduction was fixed at "a span and a half," equalling eighteen inches, though some reached a length of two feet. Nowadays the most usual length is nine inches, none often exceeding a foot. The bell should be funnel-shaped, not fashioned trumpet-wise, a clearer note being thus obtained. The quality of the note is, of course, affected by the length and diameter of the tube. From a very short Horn nothing but a discordant noise can be extracted. Probably the average Master or huntsman will obtain the best result from a nine or ten inch copper Horn with sterling or German silver mouthpiece, ferrule and bands. Horns having brass mouthpiece should be eschewed.

For a man who finds it impossible to blow the ordinary

hunting Horn, there is the Köhler Reed Horn. It looks almost exactly like the ordinary Horn, save that the ferrule is a little thicker and contains a metal tongue, and when merely breathed into produces a single note of good quality—provided the tube be of the right length. Many famous huntsmen of foxhounds, now no longer quite so sound of wind and limb as once they were, carry Reed Horns; and they are commonly used by masters of beagles and foot harriers, and sometimes of otterhounds—the exigencies of whose sport frequently finds them "out of breath" at the moment when it is most necessary to blow the Horn distinctively. With the exception of the long-swelling note recommended in *Hints to Huntsmen* to be used "to call hounds away," every "measure" given in this book can be as well—or possibly better—blown on a Reed Horn as on one of the ordinary pattern. The ear of the connoisseur may detect a slight quality of "tinniness" in the note of the former, but that is all; and there is, at any rate, no risk of unintended "discords."

III

Whichever Horn may be employed, it sounds only one note, so that the different "measures of blowing," "lessons" or "calls" can only be obtained by varying the character, length, frequency or repetition of this single note, and by the number of windes—one, two, three or four—in which the call is to be blown. It will be at once seen, therefore, that the knowledge of music required in order to read the following calls and to sound them on the Horn is of the most elementary description; being confined to the mastery of some dozen or twenty signs, all quite easily remembered. There is no need to trouble about lines and spaces, since only one note is to be sounded. In most Horns this note is D, though some sound the note of A. In the accompanying measures I have used the note D for the sake of uniformity; but, of course, it makes no difference to the calls when an A Horn is being used. All calls are given in the treble clef, about which, also, there is nothing to worry the tyro. Nor is there any trouble about bars, as no time is counted in Horn music. The vertical divisions between groups of notes indicate "windes," and simply show the points at which the performer pauses long enough to draw a fresh breath. Only five signs are employed to indicate different length of notes:—

11

The Semibreve (the longest), **O** equal to 2 minims.

The Minim, ♩ equal to 2 crotchets.

The Crotchet, ♩ equal to 2 quavers.

The Quaver, ♪ equal to 2 semiquavers; and

The Semiquaver, ♪ equal to 2 demi-semiquavers, ♬
(which are not used).

Each of these notes possesses a rest of the same duration as the note; when the Horn is silent for the same period as it would be sounded if a note occupied the position of the rest. The rests are:—

Semibreve ▬ ; Minim ▬ ;

Crotchet 𝄽 ; Quaver 𝄾 ;

Semiquaver 𝄿

A Dot after a note ● renders it half as long again.

Two Dots after a note ● ● make it three-quarters as long again.

A Pause (written as a semi-circle over the note) lengthens it.

A Dot surmounted by the Pause makes it half as long again.

These are found at the end of a winde or measure

The Staccato mark over a note mean that it is sounded sharply and abruptly.

The Legato mark or indicates that the note is a long-swelling one.

The Turn shows that the note has a trill or shake in it. It is obtained by agitating the Horn with the hand while blowing, as in the "Rattle" blown at a kill.

A vertical line on the stave indicates the end of a winde; a double vertical line at the end of the stave

shows the end of the measure.

If there are dots between the lines it signifies that the call is to be repeated.

These are all the signs of which it is necessary to have any knowledge in order to be able to read and blow Horn-music, and anyone should be able to commit them to memory in less than half-an-hour.

It may take him a little longer to learn how to sound the Horn itself, which, owing partly to its lesser length of tube, is more difficult to blow than a Post Horn. The lips of the performer should be hard, and the front teeth in good order. Hold the tube in the right hand, the bell slightly depressed, and incline it so that the wind does not blow directly into the tube. Almost close the lips, pressing them back against the teeth. Place the mouthpiece firmly against the centre of the almost closed lips and half-blow, half-spit into the mouthpiece, when a clear note should be produced. It is not necessary to puff out the cheeks, nor to discharge a lot of saliva into the Horn. Once it is found that the note can be obtained it is merely a question of practise to prolong or shorten it, so as to produce the various calls. If the beginner, after a reasonable time, finds that he is one of those not uncommon individuals who cannot and never will learn to blow a Hunting Horn, then let him fall back on a Reed Horn—which can be sounded by merely breathing straight into the mouth-piece—and thank Providence for its inventor.

It is useless attempting to blow the ordinary Horn with soft, or chapped lips, or with an aching tooth; so a Master or huntsman will always do well to have a spare Reed Horn for use in such accidental circumstances. There are many ways of carrying a Horn. The best and safest is in a leather case attached to the saddle, or when hunting on foot in a half case with leather tab fixed to the coat so that the bell protrudes between the first and second buttons.

IV

In the following collection of twenty-five Measures, Lessons and Calls for use on the Hunting Horn, I have been actuated chiefly by the desire to retrieve and restore to favour such of the old Music of the Chase as may, in my opinion, prove of practical utility in the modern hunting-field. Since pace has become the great desideratum in Quarry, Hounds and Horses, the huntsman of to-day can hardly be expected to spend time in blowing many of the elaborate calls of a long-past generation, while his fox is—in place of remaining enraptured by the musical performance in an adjacent hedgerow—as a matter of fact making with all speed for those main earths that are somehow always open. But both when throwing-off and drawing, and again at a kill or when he gets to ground, there is ample time to do justice to the musical side of the sport, and to let the unfortunates and stragglers know by means of the Horn what has been done and what is the next item on the programme. There is not a call given that need take much more than a quarter of a minutes to blow, and that surely is not a great deal to take out of a day's hunting, more especially when it operates to save many a quarter of an hour to hunt-servants and followers.

I have selected from many old works on hunting, both in French and English, and translated out of eight or ten different, and in many cases extremely quaint, systems of notation, into the simple notation of the present day—which anyone who runs or rides may read—all the purely practical measures of blowing applicable to modern hunting: ignoring those that apply to quarry—such as wolf and boar—no longer hunted in this country, and such purely fantastical measures as the "Menee," "Moots," the "Chase of the forloyng or the Perfect Chase," the measure blown "When Hounds do hunt a Game or Chase Unknown," the "Running or Farewell Recheat," and so forth.

Those I have selected are arranged in the order in which they would be naturally employed during a day's hunting: and, wherever a modern variant or substitute is in use, I have inserted it after the original call which it has supplanted. In some cases this will be found to be merely an abbreviated form of the real call: as in the case of the long doubling of the horn used when the Devon and Somerset Staghounds kill a deer, which will be found on examination to be the last winde of the original "Pryse," sounded at the taking of a stag. The modern "Rattle" used at a kill with all hounds is probably only a contracted or hurried form of this "doubling of the horn."

The first call is that "For the Company in the Morning" (I.), which I give more as a matter of curiosity and a relic of the days before hunting appointments were published, when the sportsman depended upon the note of the Horn to acquaint him with the fact that hounds were going out that day. It might be used to-day when leaving kennels, or instead of the ordinary single note to indicate that hounds are off to draw.

But for this latter purpose, the "Strake to the Field" (II.), was formerly used and might be revived. In the old days, hounds were coupled-up until they reached the covert side. The "Uncoupling" (III.), was signified by a measure in three windes, now reduced to a single monotonous note at "Throwing Off" (IV.). All these are applicable to-day to deer, fox, and otter-hunting. In hare-hunting, the proper measure to blow is "The Seek" (V.); also employable with the tufters in stag-hunting. When one cover is drawn blank and hounds go on to draw another the "Straking from Covert to Covert" (VI.), should properly be blown, as it is distinctive, and lets both hounds and field know that the huntsman is drawing on. It may be followed by the long swelling note (VII.) to call away tail hounds, and the long single note (VIII.), may still be employed to notify the whippers-in that hounds are all on and that no more are to be sought.

When the quarry is roused, whether deer, hare or fox, and when an otter is "marked," the "Veline" (IX.) is to be blown. Colonel Anstruther-Thomson's "Gone away" (X.), would seem to be a variant of the "Veline"; but the proper call on the quarry "breaking covert," is that given here to be blown in four windes (XI.). Two staccato notes (accompanied by the crack of a thong) are also noted in *Hints to Huntsmen* for use as "Tally-ho, back," and in otter-hunting may accompany the "Hark, holloa" (XII.).

The proper call when hounds are on a scent is the next given (XIII.), to be blown twice. A mere "doubling the horn" (XIV.), has taken its place to-day. With otter-hounds it may also be used when the pack has opened on a strong drag. The following lesson is that "For a fox gone to ground: if to dig" (XV.) and would prove very useful in the modern hunting-field, when many men who are not in favour of digging foxes would prefer to go home did they know what the Master's intentions were. The "Call for the Terriers at an Earth" (XVI.), too, is much wanted in these days, when great loss of time is often occasioned by the terrier-men not knowing whether their services are required or not. The sounding of this call would settle the matter in less than half a minute.

A brief and pretty lesson is that known as "To call away: if not to dig" (XVII.), and would also prove a great time-saver if universally employed. It may also be used without confusion to call hounds out of cover, instead of the long-swelling note, especially with the Reed Horn.

I now come to the lessons blown at the death of the quarry. The first is that "On the Death of a Fox," to be blown with three windes (XVIII.). According to Turbervile (1575), this might be followed by a Recheat. "The Mort of a Buck" (XIX.), was blown with two windes without a Recheat; but there were refinements, such as the "Double Moft" and the "Triple Mort," into which I need not go. "The Pryse (or Taking) of a Stag" (XX.), was celebrated "with the Recheat upon it." The first two windes are the same as in the Mort; but the third winde is the only part of the measure now used on Exmoor. In practice "The Rattle" (XXIII.), is the call nowadays blown at the death of deer, fox, hare and otter, in almost every part of the British Isles. But for the sake of variety, the following measures, "At the Worry of an Otter" (XXI), and "At the Killing of a Hare" (XXII.), might well be adopted, with the Recheat upon the latter. The Recheat is next given (XXIV.).

At the present time, when the day's sport is over and hounds are going home, it is customary for most Masters to attempt some distinctive call to notify the field of their intention. This varies in different Hunts, but usually takes the form of a few short notes followed by one more or less prolonged. The proper call is, of course, that known as "To Draw Home the Company" (XXV.), in two windes, which is so distinctive that the dullest sportsman could never mistake it for any other call.

As a contrast to these quite simple and easily-mastered calls for practical use in the modern hunting field, I give a specimen of present day French Horn music in the *fanfare de l'equipage*, called *La D'Orleans*, as used in the hunt of the

Duc de Chartres at Chantilly. All the great French Hunts have their own distinctive musical compositions, and from four to six horn-blowers are charged with their proper execution in the field. There is a healthy rivalry among these sporting musicians, and one of the attractions of the summer horse-shows in France is the competition in blowing the Compassed Horn, arranged between the representatives of the various *chasses*, in full panoply of the chase, for some prize or trophy.

I do not despair of seeing at the various hound shows held in this country at Peterborough, Reigate, and Clonmel, similar competitions open to professional and amateur huntsmen in hunt dress, for the best performance on both the ordinary and the Reed Horn, of the various measures and calls described and illustrated in this little book—the first of its sort to be offered to the public for which it is particularly intended. In this way our huntsmen may, perhaps, be induced to rise to heights at which it will be no longer possible to compare them with the beetle of the poet Collins' ode: "Winding a slow but sullen horn," without expression, variety, or any intelligible meaning. Surely from the point of view of all genuine sportsmen this were "a consummation devoutly to be wished."

No. I.-ON LEAVING KENNELS. ('Call for the Company in the Morning

No. II.-ON MOVING-OFF TO DRAW. ('The Strake to the Field'.)

2 windes.

No. III.-ON THROWING OFF. ('The Uncoupling at the Covert-side'.)

3 windes.

No. IV.-ON THROWING-OFF. (Modern.)

No. V.-'THE SEEK.' ('When Tufting, Beating for a Hare or Drawing for an Otter.)

2 windes.

No. VI.-WHEN DRAWING ON. ('Straking from Covert to Covert')

2 windes.

No. VII.-TO CALL AWAY HOUNDS.

No. VIII.-WHEN ALL AWAY. (Modern.)

No. IX.-'THE VELINE'. (On rousing the quarry or marking an otter.)

3 windes.

No. X.-'THE GONE AWAY.'

No. XI.-BREAKING COVERT.

4 windes.

No. XII.-'TALLY HO, BACK'.

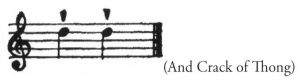

(And Crack of Thong)

No. XIII.-ON A SCENT.

To be blown twice.

No. XIV.-'DOUBLING THE HORN'.

No. XV.-FOR A FOX GONE TO GROUND: IF TO DIG.

3 windes.

No. XVI.-CALL FOR THE TERRIERS AT AN EARTH.

2 windes.

No. XVII.-TO CALL AWAY: IF NOT TO DIG.

No. XVIII.-THE DEATH OF A FOX. ('In Field or Covert.)

3 windes.

(Followed by 'The Recheat'.)

No. XIX.-'THE MORT OF A BUCK.'

2 windes.

No. XX.-'THE TAKING OF A STAG'. ✢

3 windes.

(Followed by 'The Recheat'.)

No. XXI.-AT THE WORRY OF AN OTTER.

(Followed by 'The Recheat')

No. XXII.-AT THE KILLING OF A HARE.

No. XXIII.-'THE RATTLE.' (Modern)

No. XXIV.-'THE RECHEAT'. ✦

3 windes.

No. XXV.-TO NOTIFY THE FIELD THAT HOUNDS ARE GOING HOME. ('To draw home the Company'.)

2 windes.

LA D'ORLEANS:
FANFARE DE L'ÉQUIPAGE.

(Fanfare of the Doc de Chartres' Hunt at Chantilly.)

Copied and lent for reproduction by H. A. Brydon. Esq.

✦The 'Pryse of a Hart Royal' is this Call blown thrice with three several windes.

✦A 'Royal Recheat' is this call blown thrice with three several windes.

KÖHLER & SON'S

(Sole Proprietors, SWAINE ADENEY BRIGG & SONS LTD.)

HUNTING HORNS

For many years past Messrs. KOHLER & SON have made the manufacture of Horns their *speciality*, and the greatest care is taken in the *calibre* or bore, the *mouthpiece*, and the *gauge of metal*, to ensure exactness of tone and ease in blowing; whilst by adopting the Prototype system in their construction, every Horn is a facsimile of its particular pattern, and its peculiar tone or note can be guaranteed, *whether made in Silver or Copper*.

Messrs. KOHLER & SON are the only firm possessing all the models and patterns of every Horn used by the different Masters of Hounds and Huntsmen, and have had the honour of supplying almost every Pack throughout the kingdom, as well as abroad, for a number of years past.

The patterns can be seen and a selection made at 185 PICCADILLY, where a complete Register of every Horn is kept.

COACH AND TANDEM HORNS

KOHLER'S celebrated Coach Horns have been adopted by the coaching Club, the Four-in-hand Club, the well-known Knickerbocker Club of New York; and are used by all the principal Coaches plying to and from London and throughout Great Britain and Ireland, the Continent, India, &c.

Made in the USA
Middletown, DE
07 July 2018